Essential

Green

Smoothies

© 2013 by Heartlight
P.O. Box 2251
Woodinville, WA 98072
http://ConsciouslyRaw.com

First Edition - Second Printing
ISBN 978-0-9886421-0-2
Printed in the USA

DISCLAIMER

This book is for informational purposes only and represents the opinions of the author based on her experience. It is not intended to diagnose, prescribe, or treat any illness or medical condition, nor is it intended to substitute for medical counseling. Anyone suffering from any disease, illness, or injury should consult a qualified health professional. The author and publisher of this book shall incur no liability and shall assume no responsibility to any entity or person with respect to any and all alleged loss, damage, or injury caused or alleged to be caused directly or indirectly by the information contained herein.

While every attempt has been made to verify that the information provided herein is accurate, the author assumes no responsibility for errors, inaccuracies, or omissions. The information presented in this book represents the view of the author as of the date of publication. The author reserves the right to alter her opinion based on new understanding.

Introduction from Madeline

This book is a love letter from me to you, written to inspire you with new and delicious ways to nurture your body and feed your soul. Since I believe that an improved quality of life is attainable by everyone, it is my intention to help get you started or to assist you in furthering your journey if you're already on that path.

Those of you who are interested in making positive changes in your eating habits may not know where to begin. In these pages you will discover that you can make, simply with a few chosen ingredients and a high-speed blender, delicious meals-in-a-glass that infuse your cells with plentiful nutrition. You'll discover that your body will be satisfied with less food intake than before, having received an abundance of the nutrients it needs in each rich glassful.

If you're already on the path to healthy eating, you will be delighted with the creative combination of ingredients in these recipes, chosen for their flavor, nutritional value or both. Some ingredients will be familiar, while others may be unexpected. One example is pomegranate powder, which can easily be found online or at health food stores and natural markets. Another example is wolfberries, known commercially as goji berries. Some have called the berries of this evergreen shrub a "super-food" because they are so rich in nutrients. And as you'll notice, most of the recipes are enhanced with essential oils which add an element of flavorful, aromatic pleasure.

What is a Green Smoothie?

A green smoothie is a tasty combination of fruit, leafy greens, and, in most cases, water. The alkalizing effect that these fruits and vegetables provide has been shown to be necessary for optimal health, with the leafy greens helping to restore the mineral content in our commonly-depleted bodies—a result of eating processed, acid-forming foods grown with pesticides and other chemicals in nutrient- poor soil.

General Guidelines & Helpful Hints

Since so much of what we find in our typical "standard American diet" (SAD) is devoid of vital nutrients, green smoothies are an absolutely delicious and effective way to increase our consumption of mineral-rich leafy greens. The basic formula for a green smoothie is 60% fruit to 40% leafy greens, plus water and ice. As your taste buds and your body become more accustomed to green smoothies, it is best to switch the ratios so that you move towards a mix that is higher in leafy greens. For those of you who are already seasoned green smoothie drinkers, feel free to adjust the proportions accordingly.

The recipes in this book have been tested and enjoyed but are by no means cast in stone. If there is a listed ingredient that you don't have on hand or don't prefer to use, feel free to leave it out or substitute as desired. Or you might be inspired by these suggestions to create new masterpieces of your own. In fact, I encourage it. Just be sure to write them down so that when you get a great result, you'll be able to re-create it.

Some helpful hints are worth mentioning. First, an ordinary blender will not give you the desired results. A good high-speed blender is absolutely necessary. These appliances are typically 1300- to 1500-watt units and are easily capable of pulverizing ice (or most anything). If you'd like to learn more or purchase a blender, please visit my website: **http://ConsciouslyRaw.com**.

It's a good idea to pre-soak your goji berries and dates to soften them prior to blending for a smoother result, unless of course you enjoy the occasional sweet little chunky bit. Soaking time will vary, depending on what you're working with. Finally, a word about citrus pith, the white membrane surrounding and protecting the fleshy part of the fruit: while it can be bitter in flavor, the bioflavonoids contained in the pith are known to have many health benefits. Except in the case of grapefruit, the recipes call for inclusion of the pith as the other ingredients effectively mask its strong flavor. Rest assured, these recipes do not sacrifice flavor for health.

Ingredients

Since conventional wisdom now suggests that eating a diet high in fruits and vegetables is recommended, green smoothies are a tasty and effective way to include these foods in your daily routine. It is always best to use the freshest local organic ingredients you can get your hands on as there is a commonly held belief in holistic circles that dis-ease is caused by two factors: toxicity and deficiency. As you decrease your consumption of dead, processed, and/or chemical-laden food, and increase your intake of fresh organic produce, nuts and seeds, the body responds with gratitude. Your cells are nourished and fed, and you begin to feel more energetic and alive. Your skin begins to glow, cravings vanish, and unwanted pounds seemingly melt away.

All you have to do is look at the state of health care in our world right now and it is evident that there is much room for improvement. Eating denatured food that has been grown in depleted soil or has been genetically altered and/or processed is quite commonplace. Add to that the chemical fertilizers, pesticides and the host of other chemicals and heavy metals we are being bombarded with on a daily basis, and it's no wonder that there are so many life-threatening diseases on the rise.

About Essential Oils

I first began using essential oils about 15 years ago and found them to be extremely effective in supporting physical and emotional well being in myself and in those with whom I worked. The "essential oil" of a plant is its life-blood and contains a variety of anti-viral, anti-bacterial, anti-inflammatory, and infection-fighting properties which help to keep the plant healthy. The use of essential oils to support optimal health is well documented, and dates back to Egyptian times, thousands of years B.C. It was a natural progression for me to combine my passion for these gifts from nature with my desire to support a lifestyle of health and well-being. In addition to their healthful properties, you will find that essential oils enhance the flavor of your smoothie creations in delightful ways you might not have anticipated.

The quality of essential oils and the methods by which they are extracted varies greatly from one manufacturer to the next. Because the oils are to be ingested, it is necessary to use only independently tested and certified "therapeutic grade" products which are 100% pure and free of pesticides, contaminants, synthetic chemicals, and fillers. Never ingest any oil that has not been approved for dietary consumption by the Food and Drug Administration (FDA).

Many of my recipes contain options for using a drop or two of an essential oil or a fresh fruit equivalent, however in a few cases, a blend of oils is recommended and instructions are provided. I found that the addition of these blends added an unexpected and welcomed depth of flavor and interest. These blends, as well as the individual oils, are available commercially. For information or to place an order, please visit: **http://ConsciouslyRaw.com/oils**.

Acknowledgements

A project like this book can only happen with the support of a number of dedicated and loving souls who provide the inspiration and energy needed to make a dream into a reality. I would like to acknowledge some of them here.

To Mark, my beloved husband and partner, I offer my deep appreciation for your continued love and support. This book would still be a dream without the countless hours you spent researching and editing the material in addition to all the technical support. I could not have done it without you, and I feel blessed to be sharing this life with you.

To my talented artist and friend Royce Richardson, who I am sure after the world sees his beautiful work will no longer be what has felt to me like a well-kept secret, I express my deep appreciation. It was Royce who originally suggested that the book could be a fully-illustrated work rather than just text and photographs. In addition to his talent as an illustrator, Royce is also an accomplished composer, an award-winning author and is extremely proficient at a variety of other artistic expressions. His endless well of creativity never ceases to amaze me.

To my friend and teacher, Dr. DiVanna Vadree, thank you for continually reminding me who I am and for helping me to clear away the flotsam and jetsam that has kept me hiding out and playing small.

To Victoria Boutenko, whose research led to the discovery of the green smoothie concept, I thank you from the bottom of my heart. You changed my life, and now I'm paying it forward.

To my mentor, Karen Knowler, thank you for your wisdom, encouragement, and generosity of spirit.

To you, the reader, I honor you for taking steps to enhance or restore your vitality. It is a journey like no other.

Contents

Apple

It has been said that long ago in Cumberland, England, folks would roast apples by hanging them from strings over the hearth. Once roasted the apple bits would find their way into a bowl of mulled cider that awaited below.

The malic and tartaric acids in apples, along with their high fiber content, make them easily digestible. Their flavonoid and anti-oxidant content is said to improve immune function. Apples also have pectin, which can favorably affect cholesterol and blood sugar levels.

Simply Delicious

1 apple, cored and cut into pieces

1 banana, fresh or frozen

1 bunch fresh spinach leaves, lower stems removed

2 drops lemon essential oil or 1/2 fresh lemon, seeds removed, pith on

12 ounces purified water

6–8 ice cubes

Place purified water, fruit, greens, essential oil or fresh lemon and ice in your high-speed blender. Blend until smooth and enjoy!

Samoa Surf

1 apple, cored and cut into pieces

1 pear, stem and seeds removed

1 nectarine

1 bunch golden beet greens

1 small handful sorrel

2 drops grapefruit essential oil or 1/4 fresh
 grapefruit

12 ounces purified water

6–8 ice cubes

Place purified water, fruit, greens, essential
oil or fresh grapefruit and ice in your high-
speed blender. Blend until smooth and enjoy!

ふ　ふ　ふ　ふ　ふ

Surprisingly, hundreds of years ago, sorrel was a
commonly used ingredient in a variety of recipes.
Its popularity is on the rise today and its lemony
flavor is being enjoyed anew. The leaves of the
younger plants are preferred, as the older ones
become bitter in flavor with age.

&a &a &a &a &a

Romaine lettuce contains a relatively high percentage of Omega-3 fatty acids, making it an excellent vegetarian source of these essential nutrients. They are considered "essential" because the body cannot synthesize them on its own but they are vital for normal metabolism.

Green Apple Pie

2 apples, cored and cut into pieces

6 romaine lettuce leaves

1 tablespoon date paste*

1/4 teaspoon apple pie spice**

2 drops lemon essential oil or 1/2 lemon, seeds
  removed, pith on

12 ounces purified water

6–8 ice cubes

*Soak 1 cup of pitted medjool dates in 1 cup of warm
  water until they begin to soften, then blend
  together in your high-speed blender. Freeze unused
  portion or store in fridge for up to one week.

**2 parts ground cinnamon, 1 part ground nutmeg,
  1/2 part ground cardamom

Place purified water, fruit, greens, date paste, spice,
essential oil or fresh lemon, and ice in your
high-speed blender. Blend until smooth and enjoy!

Sea captains who once sailed trade routes in the West Indies often refused to haul crates of bananas. Why? There was a well-known superstition that ships carrying bananas in their cargo often experienced great hardships at sea and sometimes never returned
from their voyage.

Bananas are high in potassium, a compound that helps brain function and learning. If you're a student, try eating a banana before your next exam!

Banana

Banana Float

1 banana, cut into small pieces (preferably frozen)

1 cup blueberries (fresh or frozen)

1 bunch beet greens

1/2 fresh lemon, seeds removed, pith on or 2 drops
   pure lemon essential oil

12 ounces purified water

6–8 ice cubes (or less if fruit is frozen)

Place purified water, fruit, greens, fresh lemon or
essential oil and ice in your high-speed blender. Blend
until smooth and enjoy!

Jungle Juice

1 small frozen banana

1 cup frozen cherries

2 handfuls baby mixed greens

1 drop lime essential oil or 1/4 fresh lime, including pith

16 ounces purified water (adjust for desired thickness)

6–8 ice cubes

Place purified water, fruit, greens, essential oil or fresh lime and ice in your high-speed blender. Blend until smooth and enjoy!

Hang loose . . . it's a jungle out there.

❧ ❧ ❧ ❧ ❧

The unique combination of nutrients in
bananas increases serotonin levels. The body uses
serotonin to regulate mood, appetite, and sleep.

Verde Tropicale

1 orange, peeled, pith on

1 banana, cut into small pieces (preferably frozen)

1 cup mango, fresh or frozen

4 large chard leaves

2 drops lime essential oil or 1/4 fresh lime, seeds removed, pith on

12 ounces purified water

6–8 ice cubes (or less if fruit is frozen)

Place purified water, fruit, greens, essential oil or fresh lime and ice in your high-speed blender. Blend until smooth and enjoy!

You'll think you're on
holiday in the tropics!

🐚 🐚 🐚 🐚 🐚

Swiss chard, like other leafy green vegetables, is
an excellent source of calcium, which helps to
strengthen the bones and teeth. It also contains
vitamin K and magnesium, both of which are
important for strong bones.

Blackberries originated in Europe and are considered a noxious weed in New South Wales. Their name comes from bramble, which means "prickly."

Blackberries are high in a bioflavonoid known as anthocyanin which is thought to be supportive of liver and memory function and healthy vision, to name just a few of its potential benefits.

Blackberry

Blackberry Stinger

1 banana, cut into small pieces (preferably frozen)

1 cup blackberries

1/2 apple, cored and cut into pieces

2 large handfuls spinach, lower stems removed

2 drops lemon essential oil or 1/2 fresh lemon, seeds removed, pith on

12 ounces purified water

6–8 ice cubes

Place purified water, fruit, greens, essential oil or fresh lemon and ice in your high-speed blender.

Blend until smooth and enjoy!

Beet greens are one my favorite leafy greens for smoothies. Their flavor is mild and delicious and they can be used in any recipe where spinach is called for. Beet tops have more nutritional value than the root, which is ironic given that most people consume the root and discard the leaves!

Healthy Harvest

1 apple, cored and cut into pieces

6 plums

1 cup blackberries

1 bunch beet greens

1 drop lemon essential oil or 1/2 fresh lemon, seeds removed, pith on

1 drop lime essential oil or 1/2 fresh lime, seeds removed, pith on

12 ounces purified water

6–8 ice cubes

Place purified water, fruit, greens, essential oils or fresh lemon, lime and ice in your high-speed blender. Blend until smooth and enjoy!

Blueberry

Once in a Blue Moon Brew

2 cups blueberries, fresh or frozen

1 pear, stem and seeds removed

2 large handfuls mache (lamb's lettuce)

1 small handful micro greens or sprouts

2 drops pure lemon essential oil or 1/2 fresh lemon, seeds removed, pith on

12 ounces purified water

6–8 ice cubes

Place purified water, fruit, greens, essential oil or fresh lemon and ice in your high-speed blender. Blend until smooth and enjoy!

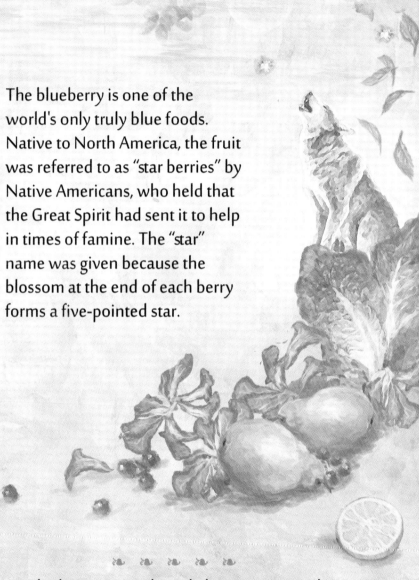

The blueberry is one of the world's only truly blue foods. Native to North America, the fruit was referred to as "star berries" by Native Americans, who held that the Great Spirit had sent it to help in times of famine. The "star" name was given because the blossom at the end of each berry forms a five-pointed star.

❧ ❧ ❧ ❧ ❧

Blueberries are relatively low in sugar and loaded with vitamins, minerals, antioxidants and phytochemicals, making them a better choice for anyone on a low-glycemic diet.

Antioxidants in blueberries have been shown to
neutralize harmful by-products of metabolism
known as "free radicals," which if unchecked
have the potential to contribute to a variety of
illnesses.

Blueberry Fountain

1 cup blueberries, fresh or frozen

1 large apple, cored and cut into pieces

1 kiwi, skin on

4 large leaves rainbow chard

2 drops lime essential oil or 1/4 fresh lime, seeds
   removed, pith on

12 ounces purified water

6–8 ice cubes

Place purified water, fruit, greens, essential oil or
fresh lime and ice in your high-speed blender.
Blend until smooth and enjoy!

Cherries appear in folklore where they have been linked to the cuckoo bird. An old Scottish proverb tells the story of a cuckoo that ceases its singing only after it has eaten three good meals of cherries.

Cherries are one of the few sources of dietary melatonin, a powerful antioxidant. Melatonin helps synchronize the body's natural rhythms, including sleep cycles.

Cherry

Cuckoo for Cherries

- 2 cups cherries, pitted (Rainiers work especially well)
- 1 banana, peeled, cut into pieces (preferably frozen)
- 1 large handful baby kale
- 2 drops orange essential oil
- 12 ounces purified water
- 6–8 ice cubes

Place purified water, fruit, greens, essential oil and ice in your high-speed blender. Blend until smooth and enjoy!

The 33% increase in the consumption of spinach in the United States that occurred in the 1930's has been accredited to Popeye, who was perhaps its most famous consumer.

Bahama Breeze

1/4 pineapple, cut into pieces including core, outer skin removed

2 cups frozen cherries

2 large handfuls spinach, lower stems removed

1 thumbnail-size piece of fresh ginger

2 drops lemon essential oil or 1/2 fresh lemon, seeds removed, pith on

12 ounces purified water

6–8 ice cubes

Place purified water, fruit, greens, ginger, essential oil or fresh lemon and ice in your high-speed blender. Blend until smooth and enjoy!

Ancient Romans considered Venus to be the goddess of fertility. According to folklore, the lime tree was considered a female tree and was believed to be helpful for fertility issues.

Lime is high in vitamin C and flavonoids and is extremely beneficial in both cleansing and nourishing the body. It is prized for its versatility in culinary creations and personal care products alike.

Citrus

Green Goddess

2 large sweet apples, cored and cut into pieces

1 stalk celery, including leaves

1 cup fresh parsley, lower stems removed

2 large chard leaves, including stems

2 drops lemon essential oil or 1/2 fresh lemon, seeds removed, pith on

2 drops lime essential oil or 1/4 fresh lime, seeds removed, pith on

1 thumbnail-size piece of fresh ginger

12 ounces purified water

6—8 ice cubes

Place purified water, fruit, greens, essential oils or fresh lemon, lime, ginger and ice in your high-speed blender. Blend until smooth and enjoy!

Orange at the Oasis

1 orange, peeled, pith on

1 apple, cored and cut into pieces

1 bunch beet greens

1 large chard leaf

1/2 teaspoon vanilla extract

1 drop citrus essential oil blend

12 ounces purified water

6–8 ice cubes

Place purified water, fruit, greens, vanilla, essential oil and ice in your high-speed blender. Blend until smooth and enjoy!

You can "brew" your own citrus blend by combining orange, lemon, grapefruit, mandarin, and tangerine essential oils.

Aromatherapists often turn to the essential oil of
the grapefruit because of its uplifting qualities.
When diffused in a room, grapefruit oil creates a
relaxed environment conducive to balanced
emotions and the relief of stress.

Citrus Bouquet

1 grapefruit, most of pith removed (unless you like bitter flavor)

1 apple, cored and cut into pieces

1 large handful beet greens

1 small handful fresh parsley leaves

1/2 teaspoon vanilla extract

2 drops citrus essential oil blend (see p. 28)

12 ounces purified water

6–8 ice cubes

Place purified water, fruit, greens, vanilla, essential oil blend and ice in your high-speed blender. Blend until smooth and enjoy!

A Philippine legend states that the human race originated from two coconuts washed up by the sea onto a sandy shore.

❧ ❧ ❧ ❧ ❧

For decades, experts have extolled the benefits of a low-fat diet. The current belief within the scientific community is quite different: a moderate amount of healthy fats accompanying a healthy diet is thought to be best.

Coconut

Put 'da Lime in 'da Coconut

1 apple, cored and cut into pieces

1/4 pineapple, cut into pieces including core, outer skin removed

1 bunch beet greens

1 small handful cilantro, lower stems removed

1/2 cup young Thai coconut meat

3 drops lime essential oil or
   1/2 fresh lime, seeds removed, pith on

12 ounces coconut water

6–8 ice cubes

Place coconut water, fruit, greens, coconut meat, cilantro, essential oil or fresh lime and ice in your high-speed blender. Blend until smooth and enjoy!

Paradise Found

1/3 pineapple, cut into pieces including core, outer skin removed

1/2 mango

2 large handfuls baby chard

1/2 cup meat from a young Thai coconut

2 drops lime essential oil or 1/4 fresh lime, seeds removed, pith on

12 ounces coconut water

6–8 ice cubes

Place coconut water, fruit, greens, lime or essential oil and ice in your high-speed blender. Blend until smooth and enjoy!

❧ ❧ ❧ ❧ ❧

Coconut water is a very potent source of electrolytes and natural sugar. As its pH is nearly identical to human plasma, soldiers have been given coconut water IVs for rehydration in wartime emergencies.

Dandelion

Maddy's Home Brew

2 bananas, peeled, cut into small pieces
   (preferably frozen)

1 bunch golden beet greens

1 small handful dandelion greens

2 drops orange essential oil

12 ounces coconut water

8 ounces purified water

6–8 ice cubes

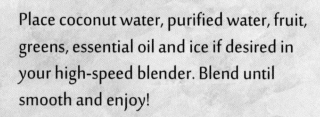

Place coconut water, purified water, fruit,
greens, essential oil and ice if desired in
your high-speed blender. Blend until
smooth and enjoy!

Many homes have dandelions growing in the garden, which are often treated like weeds. Dandelions are actually a very nutritious survival food. If you can't beat 'em, eat 'em!

A common ingredient in many detox regimens, dandelion greens are often used to cleanse the liver, making them perfect for some inner "spring cleaning" after a winter of eating heavier foods.

Lion's Roar

1 cup blackberries

1/2 apple, cored and cut into pieces

1 kiwi, skin on

1 large handful spinach, lower stems removed

1 small handful dandelion greens

2 drops grapefruit essential oil

12 ounces purified water

6–8 ice cubes

Place purified water, fruit, greens, essential oil and ice in your high-speed blender. Blend until smooth and enjoy!

Put a little roar into your meow!

Blackberries are an excellent source of
vitamin K, which is used by the body for the clotting
of blood and to aid in the absorption of calcium.

Dandy at Dawn

1 apple, cored and cut into pieces

1/2 large mango

3 large Swiss chard leaves, stems included

1 small handful dandelion greens

2 drops grapefruit essential oil or 1/4 fresh
   grapefruit

16 ounces purified water

6—8 ice cubes

Place purified water, fruit, greens, essential oil
and ice in your high-speed blender. Blend
until smooth and enjoy!

፨ ፨ ፨ ፨ ፨

Often discarded as kitchen scraps, Swiss chard stems
are rich in L-glutamine, an immune-boosting amino
acid that supports the body in recovering from surgery
and injuries.

Siddhārtha Gautama, also known as the Buddha, is said to have achieved enlightenment while sitting underneath the Bodhi, an ancient and revered fig tree.

Figs are an excellent source of minerals and fiber, and contain an abundance of calcium, magnesium, iron, copper and manganese. Ten dried figs contain about as much calcium as a cup of whole milk.

Fig

Buddha's Delight

2 oranges, peeled, pith on

6 fresh figs

4 chard leaves

1/4 teaspoon vanilla extract

2 drops lime essential oil or 1/4 fresh lime,
    seeds removed, pith on

12 ounces purified water

6–8 ice cubes

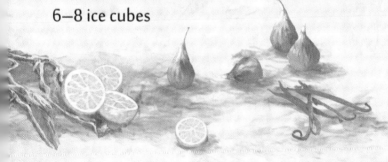

Place purified water, fruit, greens, vanilla, essential
oil or fresh lime and ice in your high-speed blender.
Blend until smooth and enjoy!

Quan Yin's Garden

1 apple, cored and cut into pieces

1 cup frozen cherries

1 bunch beet greens

3 figs

1 small handful edible flower petals

12 ounces water

6–8 ice cubes

Place purified water, fruit, greens, flower petals and ice in your high-speed blender. Blend until smooth and enjoy!

තa තa තa තa තa

Fig trees were believed to symbolize sweetness,
fertility, and abundance. Although the fig is generally
considered to be a fruit, the fruit is actually its seeds.

For centuries, fishermen have been known to chew on a slug of ginger in rough seas to ward off seasickness. It is said that rubbing ginger on a wart can cause it to disappear in a matter of days.

The use of ginger has been approved for pregnancy-related nausea and vomiting and motion sickness in Germany's *Commission E* monographs, a comprehensive therapeutic guide to herbal medicine.

Ginger

Thai Ginger

1 large apple, cored and cut into pieces

1/2 mango

1 bunch beet greens

1 thumbnail-size piece of ginger

1 drop lemongrass essential oil

16 ounces purified water

6–8 ice cubes

Place purified water, fruit, greens, ginger,
essential oil and ice in your high-speed blender.
Blend until smooth and enjoy!

In Roman times, rocket was thought to have
aphrodisiac qualities. Some claim that it was
for this reason the cultivation of rocket was
forbidden in monasteries.

Ginger Hopper

2 large sweet apples, cored and cut into pieces

4 large leaves green chard

1 small handful rocket (arugula)

1 small thumbnail-size piece ginger

5 drops orange essential oil

12 ounces purified water

6 -8 ice cubes

Place purified water, fruit, greens, ginger, essential oil and ice in your high-speed blender. Blend until smooth and enjoy!

The grape harvest has been associated with fertility deities, including Egypt's Hathor, the Goddess of joy, music and dance!

Worldwide, there are at least 60 species and 8,000 or more varieties of grapes. Since grapes contain about 80% water, they are considered to be a good low-calorie snack.

Grape

Hathor's Joy

30 grapes

1/4 pineapple, cut into pieces including core, outer skin removed

2 large handfuls spinach, lower stems removed

1 thumbnail-size piece of ginger

2 drops lemon essential oil or 1/2 fresh lemon, seeds removed, pith on

2 drops lime essential oil or 1/4 fresh lime, seeds removed, pith on

12 ounces purified water

6–8 ice cubes

Place purified water, fruit, greens, ginger, essential oils or fresh lemon or lime and ice in your high-speed blender. Blend until smooth and enjoy!

Nectar of the Vine

2 cups grapes

2 cups mixed berries, fresh or frozen

4 chard leaves with stems

1 small handful watercress

2 drops lemon essential oil, or 1/2 fresh lemon,
   seeds removed, pith on

12 ounces purified water

6–8 ice cubes

Place purified water, fruit, greens, essential oil
or fresh lemon and ice in your high-speed
blender. Blend until smooth and enjoy!

Grapes are helpful in alkalizing the blood and
hydrating the body and their high nutritional
value is undisputed.

Because the Ancient Greeks thought that Hercules wore a garland of parsley, they crowned war heroes and the winners of contests with garlands of the herb in honor of his great feats. It is said that Greek soldiers fed parsley to their horses so they would run better.

Parsley is more than just a garnish! This nutrient-rich herb is an excellent source of potassium, calcium, iron and manganese, and is believed to be especially supportive of the bones and the adrenal glands.

Greens, Herbs & Sprouts

Crowning Glory

2 apples, cored and cut into pieces

1 orange, peeled, pith on

2 stalks celery, leaves included

1 handful parsley, lower stems removed

1 leaf lacinato kale

1 small or 1/2 large avocado

2 drops lime essential oil or 1/4 fresh lime, seeds removed, pith on

12 ounces purified water

6—8 ice cubes

Place purified water, fruit, greens, essential oil or fresh lime and ice in your high-speed blender. Blend until smooth and enjoy!

❧ ❧ ❧ ❧ ❧

Spinach is listed among the fruits and vegetables
deemed most susceptible to pesticide contamination.
The Environmental Working Group recommends that
consumers reduce their exposure by always seeking
out organic varieties.

I Eats Me Spinach

1/3 pineapple, cut into pieces including core, outer skin removed

1 bunch fresh spinach, lower stems removed

1 handful cilantro, lower stems removed

1 thumbnail-size piece fresh ginger or a drop of ginger essential oil*

12 ounces purified water

6—8 ice cubes

*Note: the ginger essential oil is highly concentrated and will result in a much stronger flavor.

Place purified water, fruit, greens, ginger or essential oil and ice in your high-speed blender. Blend until smooth and enjoy!

In the Middle Ages, cinnamon was affordable only to the very wealthy. The number and amount of spices a person could afford was a measure of their social status.

Over the Rainbow

1 peach

1 cup grapes

3 large leaves rainbow chard with stems

1 large handful baby kale

*2 drops metabolic essential oil blend

12 ounces purified water

6–8 ice cubes

*The metabolic blend can be made by combining grapefruit, lemon, ginger, peppermint, and cinnamon essential oils.

Place purified water, fruit, greens, essential oil and ice in your high-speed blender. Blend until smooth and enjoy!

Raspberries are low in calories and saturated fats
and are a deliciously rich source of antioxidants and
dietary fiber.

Peas-full Garden

1 apple, cored and cut into pieces

1/2 cup raspberries

2 large handfuls pea vines

2 tablespoons goji berries (pre-soaked)

2 drops tangerine essential oil

16 ounces purified water

6—8 ice cubes

Place purified water, fruit, greens, essential oil and ice in your high-speed blender. Blend until smooth and enjoy!

Smooth Sailing

2 Bartlett pears, stem and seeds removed

1 apple, cored and cut into pieces

6 medium-sized collard leaves

1 handful cilantro, lower stems removed

1 thumbnail-size piece fresh ginger or
   1 drop ginger essential oil*

12 ounces purified water

6—8 ice cubes

*Note: the ginger essential oil is highly concentrated and will result in a much stronger flavor.

Place purified water, fruit, greens, fresh ginger or essential oil and ice in your high-speed blender. Blend until smooth and enjoy!

❧ ❧ ❧ ❧ ❧

In addition to their use in green smoothies, collard leaves make a great sandwich wrap. I often enjoy mine filled with sunflower seed paté or assorted fresh vegetables. They are a great low-calorie gluten-free substitute for bread.

Sunshine Shake

2 pears, stem and seeds removed

2 handfuls Chinese spinach

1 small handful sunflower sprouts

1 drop tangerine essential oil

12 ounces purified water

6–8 ice cubes

Place purified water, fruit, greens, sprouts, essential oil and ice in your high-speed blender. Blend until smooth and enjoy!

Considered a "living" food, sunflower sprouts are packed with vitamins and minerals. Beyond their use as a green smoothie additive, they are delicious on salads, in wraps, or all by themselves. You can grow them easily yourself indoors in about a week's time.

æ æ æ æ æ

Orange essence is simultaneously uplifting and
calming to the mind, body and spirit. Whether
you add it to your smoothie or include a drop or
two in your bath water, you'll be enlivened by its
sweet fragrance.

The Kitchen Sink

12 grapes

1 apple, cored and cut into pieces

1 bunch spinach, lower stems removed

1 small handful parsley, lower stems removed

1 drop orange essential oil

12 ounces purified water

6–8 ice cubes

Place purified water, fruit, greens, essential oil and ice in your high-speed blender. Blend until smooth and enjoy!

Kiwi fruit was originally called Chinese gooseberry and is native to Southern China. Exporters renamed it kiwi after the fruit's resemblance to New Zealand's national symbol, the flightless kiwi bird, and because it was thought to be a more marketable name.

Kiwi skin is loaded with anti-oxidants and fiber. Just cut it into a few chunks and pop it in the blender, or eat it plain if you don't mind the fuzziness.

Kiwi Fruit

Kiwi Magic

1/3 pineapple, cut into pieces including core, outer
   skin removed

2 kiwis, ends trimmed, skin on

1 bunch beet greens

1 small handful cilantro, lower stems removed

2 drops lime essential oil or 1/4 fresh lime, seeds
   removed, pith on

12 ounces purified water

6—8 ice cubes

Place purified water, fruit, greens, essential oil or
fresh lime and ice in your high-speed blender. Blend
until smooth and enjoy!

According to Hindu legend, an evil sorceress incinerated the sun princess and a mango tree sprouted and grew from her ashes. The Emperor was enchanted with the mango flower and the intensity of his love transformed it back into the princess. The two lived happily thereafter.

Mangoes are prized for their culinary versatility, delicious when incorporated into any meal from breakfast to dessert, and everything in between.

Mango

Mango Majesty

- 2 manila mangoes
- 1 apple, cored and cut into pieces
- 4 chard leaves
- 2 drops lemon essential oil or 1/2 fresh lemon, seeds removed, pith on
- 12 ounces purified water
- 6–8 ice cubes

Place purified water, fruit, greens, essential oil or fresh lemon and ice in your high-speed blender. Blend until smooth and enjoy!

Mango Mirage

3 manila mangoes (small yellow)

1/2 banana

2 cups spinach, lower stems removed

1/4 cup cilantro, lower stems removed

2 drops lemon essential oil or 1/4 fresh lemon, seeds removed, pith on

12 ounces purified water

6–8 ice cubes

Place purified water, fruit, greens, essential oil or fresh lemon and ice in your high-speed blender. Blend until smooth and enjoy!

Did you know that the mango is related (distantly) to the cashew and pistachio? One of the most popular fruits internationally, most of the world's mangoes are grown in India, which consumes more than it exports.

Some people strongly dislike cilantro, saying it tastes like soap, while others greatly enjoy the flavor. Added to your green smoothie, whichever camp you fall in, you may be pleasantly surprised at the result.

Catch of the Day

1/4 pineapple, cut into pieces including core, outer skin removed

1 manila mango

1 bunch beet greens

1 small handful cilantro, lower stems removed

1 thumbnail-size piece ginger

2 drops lime essential oil or 1/4 fresh lime, seeds removed, pith on

12 ounces purified water

6–8 ice cubes

Place purified water, fruit, greens, ginger, essential oil or fresh lime and ice in your high-speed blender. Blend until smooth and enjoy!

Valued for its cleansing properties since ancient times, watercress is a member of the mustard family. Irish monks were said to survive for long periods subsisting on only bread and watercress. They considered the leaf to be "pure food for sages."

Rainforest Fantasy

1 apple, cored and cut into pieces

1/2 mango

1 large handful sorrel

1 small handful watercress

1 tablespoon pomegranate powder

2 drops lemon essential oil or 1/2 fresh lemon, seeds removed, pith on

12 ounces purified water

6–8 ice cubes

Place purified water, fruit, greens, pomegranate powder, essential oil or fresh lemon and ice in your high-speed blender. Blend until smooth and enjoy!

Peach

Just Peachy

2 large juicy peaches

1 bunch beet greens

1/4 teaspoon vanilla extract

2 drops orange essential oil

12 ounces almond milk

6—8 ice cubes

Place almond milk, fruit, greens, vanilla, essential oil and ice in your high-speed blender. Blend until smooth and enjoy!

According to ancient Japanese legend, Momotarō, the "peach boy," arrived on Earth inside a giant peach. An elderly couple found the peach floating down the river and discovered the child when they tried to open the peach to eat it. The boy told them that he had been sent from Heaven to be their son. They named him Momotarō, a combination of momo (peach) and tarō (eldest son).

Years later, after his village was attacked by demons, Momotarō fought the invaders on their distant island. On his quest, he met and befriended a talking dog, a monkey, and a pheasant, who agreed to help him.

Peachy Fiesta

2 ripe juicy peaches

1 kiwi, including skin

2 large handfuls spinach, lower stems removed

2 drops lemon essential oil or 1/2 fresh lemon,
  seeds removed, pith on

2 drops lime essential oil or 1/4 fresh lime,
  seeds removed, pith on

12 ounces purified water

6—8 ice cubes

Place purified water, fruit, greens, essential
oils or fresh lemon, lime and ice in your high-
speed blender. Blend until smooth and enjoy!

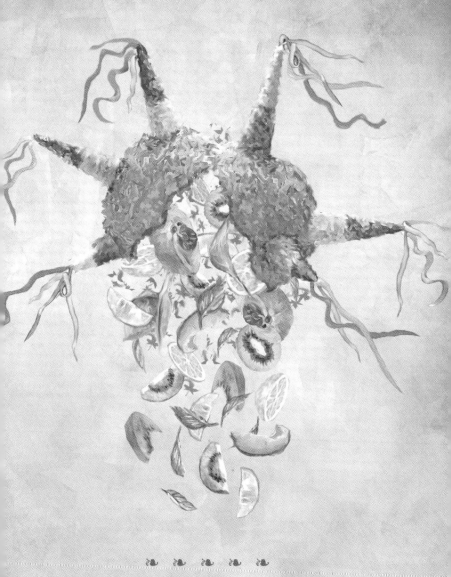

⁜ ⁜ ⁜ ⁜ ⁜

Although peaches should be kept refrigerated for freshness, they taste sweeter when consumed at room temperature. Consider leaving one out on the kitchen counter before going to bed for use in your morning smoothie.

🐌 🐌 🐌 🐌 🐌

When choosing salad greens, those with the darker
green leaves are the most nutritious. With such a wide
variety of choices available in the marketplace, be
sure to vary your selection, opting for the freshest
organic produce you can find.

Nectar of the Gods

2 peaches

1 cup strawberries, including hulls

2 large handfuls mixed salad greens

2 drops lemon essential oil or 1/2 fresh lemon,
   seeds removed, pith on

12 ounces purified water

6–8 ice cubes

Place purified water, fruit, greens, essential oil or
fresh lemon and ice in your high-speed blender.
Blend until smooth and enjoy!

Take the plunge!

In China, the peach tree was considered the "tree of life,"
as peaches symbolize unity and immortality. Images of
peaches are used to attract good health and long life.

Peach Plunge

1 peach

1 nectarine

1 cup strawberries, fresh or frozen

1 handful spinach, lower stems removed

1 kale leaf

1 collard leaf

3 drops lemon essential oil or 1/2 fresh lemon, seeds removed, pith on

12 ounces purified water

6–8 ice cubes

Place purified water, fruit, greens, essential oil or fresh lemon and ice in your high-speed blender. Blend until smooth and enjoy!

What a Pear

- 2 Bartlett pears, stem and seeds removed
- 1/3 bunch parsley, lower stems removed
- 3 large chard leaves
- 2 drops lemon essential oil or 1/2 fresh lemon, seeds removed, pith on
- 12 ounces purified water
- 6—8 ice cubes

Place purified water, fruit, greens, essential oil or lemon and ice in your high-speed blender. Blend until smooth and enjoy!

The Russians believed that placing a pear around the neck of a cow would offer it protection. Pears were described by Homer in "The Odyssey" as "a gift of the gods."

Pears should always be picked before they are
fully ripened, otherwise they can become gritty
and less flavorful.

Pears need to ripen at room temperature. You can speed up the process by placing them in a paper bag or slow it down by refrigerating them.

Perfect Pear

1 pear, stem and seeds removed

1 orange, including pith, outer skin removed

4 large chard leaves

2 drops lemon essential oil, or 1/2 fresh lemon, seeds removed, pith on

12 ounces purified water

6–8 ice cubes

Place purified water, fruit, greens, essential oil or fresh lemon and ice in your high-speed blender. Blend until smooth and enjoy!

Persimmon

Persimmon in the Wind

1 ripe Fuyu persimmon, top removed, cut into pieces

2 Bartlett pears, stem and seeds removed

1 bunch beet greens

2 drops lemon essential oil, or 1/2 fresh lemon, seeds removed, pith on

12 ounces purified water

6—8 ice cubes

Place purified water, fruit, greens, essential oil or fresh lemon and ice in your high-speed blender. Blend until smooth and enjoy!

The watermelon-sized seeds in the mushy, ripe persimmon can predict the severity of the upcoming winter, according to Ozark folk wisdom. If the split seeds are spoon-shaped, much shoveling of snow is ahead, fork shapes indicate light snowfall, while knife shapes foretell cutting cold winds.

Persimmons contain important nutrients including potassium, magnesium, calcium, iron and manganese.

When choosing persimmons, they should be firm to the touch and the skin should be shiny, blemish-free, and deep orange in color. They ripen quickly at room temperature and should be eaten promptly or refrigerated for up to three days.

91

Smoothie by the Sea

2 Fuyu persimmons, tops removed, cut into
   pieces

1 apple, cored and cut into pieces

2 large handfuls spinach, lower stems removed

1 thumbnail-size piece of fresh ginger

1/2 teaspoon vanilla extract

1 drop citrus essential oil blend (see p. 28)

12 ounces purified water

6–8 ice cubes

Place purified water, fruit, greens, vanilla, essential
oil and ice in your high-speed blender. Blend until
smooth and enjoy!

New England sea captains who sailed among the Caribbean Islands would return home bearing their cargo of fruits, spices and rum. The captain would mount a pineapple on a fencepost outside his home to let his friends know he was safely back from his voyage. The pineapple was an invitation for them to visit and listen to tales of his adventures.

The essential oils in the metabolic blend (grapefruit, lemon, peppermint, ginger & cinnamon) may be useful in management of hunger, calming the stomach and lifting the mood.

Pineapple

Pineapple ~ Goji

- 1/2 pineapple, including core, cut into pieces, outer skin removed
- 1/4 cup goji berries, pre-soaked to soften
- 4 large collard leaves
- 2 drops metabolic essential oil blend (see p. 58)
- 12 ounces purified water
- 6–8 ice cubes

Place purified water, fruit, greens, essential oil and ice in your high-speed blender. Blend until smooth and enjoy!

94

🐌 🐌 🐌 🐌 🐌

Pineapples originated in South America and
gained worldwide exposure and popularity as
they were transported on ships to help the sailors
to ward off scurvy.

Caribbean Cruiser

1/2 small pineapple, cut into pieces
    including core, outer skin removed

1 orange, peeled, pith on

4 lacinato kale leaves

2 large chard leaves

1 drop orange essential oil

12 ounces purified water

6–8 ice cubes

Place purified water, fruit, greens, essential oil and ice in your high-speed blender. Blend until smooth and enjoy!

Kale is a cabbage that was once known as "poor
people's food" however it is now gaining popularity
even in upscale restaurants.

Tropical Twister

1/2 small pineapple, cut into pieces including core, outer skin removed

1 kiwi, ends trimmed, skin on

1 orange, pith on

3 lacinato kale leaves

1/2 cup parsley, lower stems removed

1 drop lemongrass essential oil

12 ounces purified water

6–8 ice cubes

Place purified water, fruit, greens, essential oil and ice in your high-speed blender. Blend until smooth and enjoy!

Strawberry Salad

2 cups strawberries, fresh or frozen

1 apple, cored and cut into pieces

2 large handfuls spinach, lower stems removed

1 small handful rocket (arugula)

1 small handful parsley, lower stems removed

5 drops lime essential oil or 1/2 fresh lime, seeds removed, pith on

12 ounces purified water

6–8 ice cubes

Place purified water, fruit, greens, essential oil or fresh lime and ice in your high-speed blender. Blend until smooth and enjoy!

A Native American legend tells of how the Great Spirit created strawberries by placing them on the path of a woman who had left her husband in anger. When she stopped to taste the strawberries, their sweet flavor filled her with such joy that she forgave her husband and returned home.

Botanists do not consider strawberries to be true berries because they have their seeds on the outside, unlike (for example) blueberries and cranberries.

100

Strawberries are extremely high in fiber, which aids digestion, and proper digestion is essential for healthy immune function. It is highly recommended that you choose the organically grown variety since the absorbent nature of the strawberry makes it difficult to remove pesticides and other contaminants.

Liquid Love

1 apple, cored and cut into pieces

1 cup strawberries, fresh or frozen

1/2 large juicy ripe mango

8 romaine lettuce leaves

1/2 cup broccoli (or other) sprouts

2 drops lemon essential oil or 1/4 fresh
   lemon, seeds removed, pith on

12 ounces purified water

6–8 ice cubes

Place purified water, fruit, greens, essential oil or
fresh lemon and ice in your high-speed blender.
Blend until smooth and enjoy!

The best way to store strawberries is to place them in a fresh container on top of a folded paper towel, which will absorb any moisture that they might produce. Waiting to wash them until just prior to use will also help to preserve their freshness.

Strawberry Shortcake

2 cups strawberries, fresh or frozen

1 apple, cored and cut into pieces

2 large handfuls green chard, stems included

2 drops grapefruit essential oil or
    1/4 fresh grapefruit

12 ounces purified water

6–8 ice cubes

Place purified water, fruit, greens, essential oil and ice in your high-speed blender. Blend until smooth and enjoy!

About the Illustrator

Royce Richardson makes his home in Seattle, Washington where he designs and illustrates for several types of media, including books, film and a series of personalized videos called Luminous Meditations.

Royce's formal training includes a B.A. in Fine Arts from Seattle University. In addition to being an artist, he is also an accomplished author and composer. His novel, "The Blissmaker," was awarded a Benjamin Franklin Award for Best Work of Fiction and was also voted Book of the Year by the Coalition of Visionary Retailers. The story of his novel is not unlike his own, as it reflec the spiritual journey of a composer.

His music CD, "MoonCrest," contains piano compositions th were created throughout his writing of the novel. You can he examples of this music, and learn more about Royce's work going to **http://Blissmaker.com**.

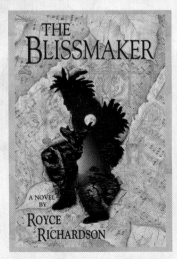

About the Author

Madeline Eyer is an internationally recognized Certified Raw Food Coach, a member of both the International Association of Raw Food Coaches & Teachers and the International Association of Women in Business Coaching.

Madeline's love of creating in the kitchen became evident decades ago when, as a pre-teen, she blew up her mom's pressure cooker. Although her chosen recipes and ingredients have evolved over time, her love of delicious, nurturing food has remained.

Her deep desire for spiritual evolution, her love of natural healing, and her sense of adventure have led Madeline to visit sacred sites on six continents, where she often furthered her acquisition of new skills.

She is well versed in a variety of holistic healing modalities and added working with essential oils to her repertoire over fifteen years ago. It was a natural progression for Madeline to combine two of her great loves: delicious, healthy food and essential oils.

Currently, Madeline resides in the Seattle area with her husband, Mark, where she teaches raw food classes and coaches clients, primarily women in mid-life, who are motivated to feel better, to have more energy, enjoy more restful sleep, and connect with their bodies at a much deeper level.

To learn more, please visit **http://ConsciouslyRaw.com**.

Recipe List